A Practical Guide to Direct Marketing Or How I Earned Half a Million Pounds in Six Months

BY
S.I.D.M.D.
J.C. Frost

ISBN: 0 946393 66 4

This book is a practical guide to direct marketing. Its purpose is to show you how you can make a fortune, without laying out a penny or taking any risks. A direct marketing business can be successful in every country, whether you live in the city or in a rural area. The author is neither an accountant nor an attorney. Both the author and S.I.D.M.D disavow any personal liability for risk or loss which could be directly or indirectly attributable to the information presented in this book.

For all legal or accounting advice, seek out professional help.

TABLE OF CONTENTS

Chapter 1
How to get rich quick

It wasn't so long ago that I was just like everybody else. When I got up in the morning, I'd wonder how I could double or triple my weekly wages. I had a regular job, but I was interested in following the example of some friends who'd managed to earn enough money to guarantee their financial independence once and for all. But there was a nagging issue to solve: what formula, concept or gadget was I going to use to get rich quick? There are millions of honest ways of earning a living. In my particular case, all I could afford to invest was my own time. Nor did I intend to borrow money to get started. I had no desire to stick my shingle up on some office door and pay $50 per square foot for the privilege. What I was looking for was a way to earn my fortune while hanging on to my job as long as necessary.

Get rid of lingering doubts

Franklin Roosevelt once explained that *today's doubts are the only things that keep us from realising tomorrow's fears*. This concept probably applies to everyone. *Doubt* and *fear* are limiting factors which keep us from taking effective action. Get rid of them. *Rely* on *yourself*. Take an inventory of your qualities. What can you do better than anyone else? Write down a list of your abilities. Think about some of your successes – those times you've been a real winner – better than the best.

Your strong points

Take a sheet of paper and jot down some of your special attributes:

- A good salesperson
- Can keep cool under pressure
- Good imagination
- Mechanical abilities
- A fantastic handyman
- A great athlete
- A good chess player

And so on. You certainly wouldn't cheat on your own test, so you can rely on the results. You probably have at least two or three strong points. It's up to you to decide with which ones you feel most comfortable and which will help you achieve your goals as quickly as possible. And if you have many strong points, you're that much further ahead already in succeeding at your projects.

A key asset: self-confidence

I have some rather pessimistic, but otherwise very talented friends. Unfortunately, they don't really succeed in life. Pessimism wipes out the qualities people need to get where they want to go. It makes you feel bitter, depressed and nervous and can even make you quite unlikeable. The pessimist only sees the bad side of life. A pessimist in New York doesn't see a Big Apple. He sees a congested, filthy, repulsive and disgusting city. After leaving a party, he puts down the other people who were there. Pessimists are in disharmony with their environment. A great philosopher once noted that: *"A man's greatest wealth is not his good fortune, but his good character."*

I have to admit that the day I decided to get into direct marketing – that is, to make money without killing myself in the process – I felt like I could do anything. Just like you can teach yourself how to be calm, you can also teach yourself how *to believe in* and *to like* yourself.

What it takes to get rich

This book isn't some kind of guide to introspection. Quite the contrary. It's the *key* that opens the door to wealth and riches. Here are the principle ingredients for success:

1) *The Concept:* Have a clear idea of the goal to be achieved and the strategy by which you intend to arrive at it.

2) *Concentration:* There are three aspects to this art: attention, self-control and continuity.

3) *Memory:* Should be developed to the maximum so that you can recall facts, figures, objects, events and people who can help you overcome your barriers.

4) *Will Power:* In working out a concept, you acquire additional information and help it grow. Your will power is bearing the fruit of your labours and will help you sustain your concept.

5) *Perseverance:* Once you've got your concept in gear, don't ever let up on the strategy without seeing it all the way through.

Fortune smiles at audacity

Some folks are terrified of everything. They're afraid of aeroplanes, thunderstorms, animals, and on and on. Any courage they might have is typically compromised by these fears. Sometimes they'll have great ideas, but fear keeps them from truly succeeding. One of my buddies, Charley, made good money with some easy work, but was *afraid* to reinvest his profits, build up his business, recruit more personnel and do what he needed to effectively quadruple his earnings. Charley was immobilised by fear. He preferred what he had to what he might have. Part of Charley's life was lost to anxiety. Fortune was within his grasp, yet he let it slip through his fingers. The moral of the story: get rid of your petty fears! Nothing ventured, nothing gained.

Direct marketing: the way to succeed

As far as I'm concerned, I know what my strong point is: resourcefulness. There are millions of other people around the world who also have the nerve, guts or initiative that often goes hand-in-hand with a good imagination. What this resourcefulness motivates me to do, above all, is earn money. Quickly and without investment. In the United States, Canada and Australia, this system of marketing directly and avoiding the middleman has been a huge success. It was the way a couple of brothers I know started out when they were students in the basement of their parents' house. They planned and built up their business little by little and it soon became a huge empire. *Direct marketing enabled these guys to earn truckloads of money.* A tremendous market was open to them and they plugged into it, using a sales approach which they made more dynamic and efficient with each passing year.

Reach the consumer directly

There are many such tales of individual success through direct marketing. I had a little bit of money saved up with which I was able to start up. That's all I needed to get my business rolling. In order to sell and reach the potential customers I targeted, I used a professional directory and sent brochures in which I succinctly described the product I wanted to sell and the advantages it offered. What I said in this brochure had *impact value*, a concept we shall discuss later on. Impact value must be ascertained in advance, because brochures cost money. So, before heading down to the printer, you'll want to make a *preliminary test*. This trial will let you know if you have to modify your promotional materials. Reprinting can be costly. Therefore it's better to polish your presentation before investing too much money.

Systems of communication

You can distribute your materials through the following channels:

- Mail
- Print (newspapers)
- Direct solicitation

Since I had a specific target group in mind, I opted for a two-step mailing process:

a) individualised letters

b) follow-up with a brochure

Obviously, this strategy made me spend more than I'd planned. As I was prospecting within a specific context, I tried to reach my potential customers using a method I call *networking*.

The secret of my success

There are a few key yet basic points which I'll explain here briefly:

• Insight

Understand the behaviour of a designated target group.

• Intuition

This means having a good feel of what's actually happening. Intuition is a product of awareness. Awareness is the essence of existence.

• Networking

This means trying to contact key individuals who are part of a network. In reality, these are the people who will sell for you. This is how the networking concept works: two friends, Mrs X and Mr Z, run into each other in the elevator. They have both received my letter in which I'm offering a particular product for sale. They discuss it and ask each other if they'll order it or not. I've got them so interested through the mail that they'll soon talk it over with other people in their particular circle. This system is more commonly known as "word of mouth".

Knowing who you're trying to reach

Before making a mass mailing, I conduct a brief analysis of a target group. This involves examining their basic impulses. I know from the start what kind of tone I'll give my letter of solicitation, what *key words* I'll use and the type of stationary it will appear on.

Know your customer

Through proper research, I try to get to understand the thought processes of my target group. All of this may seem a bit complicated at first glance, but this strategy provides extraordinary results.

Imagine, for example, that you're a sales rep for a big company. Your delicate task is to land a huge contract which is so important that the president of the firm has set up an appointment with you.

If you're a smart rep, you'll try to thoroughly gauge the situation. You'll tune into the emotional patterns of your future client. You'll know what colour he likes, if he's a good golfer, if he rides horses or what's his favourite hobby. Finding out these details will be of great assistance. Don't play on impulse. You might get lucky once, but that doesn't mean you'll be lucky all the time.

Direct marketing has evolved over the last few years. Sound preparation is required for a good mailing.

Pre-selection

In order to maximise earnings, I check out the field first by making a preliminary prospect list. Using the appropriate methods, I always try to make my product message as relevant as possible. Your copy should start off with a "hook" to capture your target's attention.

If one single element is eliminated from my system, the entire structure ends up being affected.

$10,000 per week

My first big direct marketing operation brought in $10,000 per week during the first two months. I knew there'd be a large demand for my product following the preliminary test, and I didn't hesitate investing in a broader, well targeted effort once the cash started flowing in. That's when I decided to quit my job and apply my system to different kinds of products, selling everything from gadgets to health-care items.

I was on my way. On the road to fortune.

CHAPTER 2
TEST YOUR ABILITIES

If you're a serious candidate for the *Direct Marketing* Club, you may ask yourself where to begin. This is a good question. In the first place, in order to know your abilities, you should take the following test.

QUESTION	YES	NO
• Do you like to work with figures?	☐	☐
• Do you often read newspaper and magazine ads?	☐	☐
• Do you regularly write letters to family, friends or suppliers?	☐	☐
• Are you naturally curious? Do you like the new and unusual?	☐	☐
• Do you know the basic rules of how to influence people?	☐	☐
• Do you consider yourself to be resourceful?	☐	☐
• Do you have a creative mind?	☐	☐
• Do you naturally tend to believe in yourself?	☐	☐
• Do you have any hobbies? Are you very serious about them?	☐	☐
• Are you good at dealing with money?	☐	☐
• Is your social status important to you?	☐	☐
• Do you feel well inclined to do business?	☐	☐
• Do you like to help others?	☐	☐
• Do you like money?	☐	☐
• Can you deal with problems and difficulties effectively?	☐	☐
• Do you keep an eye on your bank statement? Do you always know how much you have in your account?	☐	☐
• Can you concentrate easily?	☐	☐
• Are you often right about the motives behind people's actions?	☐	☐
• Are you a gambler?	☐	☐
• Do you like to increase your knowledge?	☐	☐
• Do you like to travel?	☐	☐

Compute your score

If you only got from *0 to 5*, this is probably not your natural field of endeavour. However, with perseverance and determination, you can overcome these handicaps. But you'll have to work hard to get into the Direct Marketing Club.

With *6 to 10*, you have some of the required attributes. But it won't be easy for you. You'll have to get to know and learn from those people who can help you in your march towards success.

With *11 to 16*, you show a sure talent for achieving your objective – success. You'll need a learning period, but once it's completed, you have a solid chance of being one of the best.

With 17 to 20, you're a natural. You have arrived at your destination. Welcome to the Direct Marketing Club. With a bit of experience, you have a real chance of making a fortune. You're a lean, mean, fightin' machine. You have some remarkable latent talents which you should realise.

The *Direct Marketing Club* is the answer to the native drive and talent you never knew you had before reading this book.

CHAPTER 3
YOU WANT TO CONQUER THE WORLD,
START FIRST WITH YOURSELF

What do you want most in the world? Why are you likely to get it through this new profession? It's simple. The test has defined your aptitudes and you've decided to put them to work for your best interests. You have the abilities which make you an ideal candidate for Direct Marketing. Without even knowing it, you simply have what it takes.

- Confidence in yourself
- Instinctive goodwill towards others
- Enthusiasm
- A set of values
- A sense of logic which gives rise to efficiency

Your test is positive. You don't have enough experience, but you will acquire it quickly. Maybe you feel you don't have enough schooling to succeed. But *never confuse practical knowledge* with *learning* or *general culture*.

I am well acquainted with folks who have three or four degrees and speak several languages, but hardly earn enough money to get by. The reason: they haven't fully developed all their abilities in a productive manner. They are not practical people.

They don't know how to put their best foot forward in order to multiply their earnings.

What do you need to succeed?

First of all, you need to show your REAL or IDEAL self. What does this mean? Here are some examples:

One person is bright, energetic and practical.

The other is not too clever, disorganised and inconsistent. If you ask him what he wants most of all on earth, he will probably answer you:

- To live well, eat well, drink well, have fun, get the most out of work and out of the other guy.

This person has no desire to realise his ideal self and doesn't understand those who, like you, get their satisfaction out of *perfectionism*.

Being in touch with your IDEAL SELF means feeling useful, thinking about things, trying to evaluate situations properly, keeping both feet on the ground and not putting off 'til tomorrow what can be done today. It also means being prosperous in your chosen field.

Self-control: the key to success

The test positively established your abilities. You have *everything you need* to succeed. You possess the basic ingredients to realise your projects.

Now you simply have to develop these assets.

How so?

You must work on your concentration and develop personal discipline. Set up a programme of goals to achieve. Study this programme and really concentrate while doing so. *Learn to think it over*, that is, you must be able to control your thoughts in order to focus your attention on one idea – the key idea which is the driving concept. This is what generates enthusiasm and leads to action.

Fix your mind on a single point. Start by concentrating according to the following system:

– 10 minutes the first day, 20 the second and progressively increase the time you concentrate on *a single subject*.

As you begin to master this exercise, you'll be astonished at the clarity with which you can dissect a problem. You will clearly see what road you should follow.

A person who *concentrates* also *thinks* intelligently. By thinking intelligently, you'll develop those resources linked to the powers in you of decision-making and accomplishment. *Accomplishing* something, in your case, means undertaking a project that you like by developing a personal strategy that enables you to push through a key idea. And to be successful doing so.

Money: a stimulus

When people ask me if I have any money, I invariably reply:

I respect it more than I like it. Money is the key to fulfilling many of our most precious dreams.

Henry Ford didn't like money for its own sake.

"What would you do if you were to lose it all one day?" a reporter once asked him.

"Well, I'd try to figure out something basic that people need and I'd be a millionaire again in a few years," he replied.

You should have the right perspective on money.

If it serves you, that's fine, but if money starts bossing you around, watch out.

You're on the wrong track.

Money is neither good or evil.

It is useful; that is all.

It's a tool for acquiring greater independence. Nothing more.

For many people who are still bound up in their Judaeo-Christian heritage, money is something to be looked down on, something filthy.

Don't spend your time putting down the rich.

Try instead to be like them.

Poverty is sometimes an open sore in an affluent society. With the enormous wealth people possess in North America, poverty can be cured.

- The spirit of initiative can enable anyone, whatever his or her origins, to overcome the frustration of poverty. Poverty is not a hereditary trait.

Some who were born into poverty have managed to amass colossal fortunes.

Conrad Hilton, the king of the hotel empire, explained to his friends that wealth is not an evil in and of itself, but the way in which it is sometimes used, is.

Soon, through your work, your initiative and your resourcefulness, you'll make considerable financial progress.

Don't feel guilty about getting rich.

Don't look down on money.

The money in your hand simply stands for the services you've provided.

I don't despise money. It's useful to me and opens doors which were shut just yesterday. I put my profits to work and I help out my family, friends and acquaintances. And each time my Direct Marketing system brings in another bundle, I congratulate myself for having earned so much money. But I don't worship it. I pass it around and buy things like art work and beautiful books, and travel as much as possible to fascinating places.

You can conquer the world with money – but only if you can conquer yourself first.

CHAPTER 4
HOW TO START YOUR OWN BUSINESS

You've made up your mind.

And you've examined the question of starting your own business thoroughly:

- Where will you set up this business?
- What will the legal status of your company be?
- Where will you get the start-up money?
- What type of stationery will you use?
- What will your logo be?
- Will you have a partner or will you go it alone?

These are some of the questions which have to be *seriously considered before* you make that big leap. Definitely not after.

In order to get going in business, you need a certain number of basic tools. You should start off by selecting the right *logo*. This can be a significant factor in your success, or lack of it.

Here is what I did. My *decision* formula applies throughout the world and has the tremendous advantage of being very realistic.

My capital

I had $80 to begin with. This was not oceans of money, but it was enough to get started. I vigorously avoided taking on debts. It's hard to work when you're weighed down with debt and it's better to start up with *limited capital* than to willy-nilly spend the money you've just borrowed from the bank or someone else.

Evidently, because of my situation, I would have been able to easily borrow a nice round sum. But I don't like mortgaging the future without knowing just what good it holds for me. I have also noted that people tend to spend money they borrow more quickly than money they earn themselves.

In short, my beginnings were modest – no fireworks.

I use one room in my apartment

Since I didn't have to see my clients, I would have been wasting money by renting an office somewhere else. Everyone knows how quickly the end of the month rolls around. My working environment was functional and inexpensive. A good work table, a filing cabinet and a telephone. Don't get a lot of extras to start up with. Little by little, your requirements will become evident. Clothes don't make a man and a fancy office is no guarantee of success. By starting modestly, and putting the emphasis on you, rather than the furniture, you'll minimise risk. There should be three key factors which determine how your facilities are organised.

- A sense of thrift
- A sense of size
- An emphasis on the functional

The money you'd spend otherwise could be better used on buying or renting client lists.

Don't bite off more than you can chew.

Organisation is like a muscle: it gets stronger the more it's used.

Company name

The selection of the right company name is crucial. How do you decide what it should be? The possibilities are endless. Your name is your coat of arms. It should have an honest ring, be short and not be funny or in any way court confusion.

Your success relies on making the right choice. Consider the context in which you will be operating. Many names work well in more than one language. This is particularly important if you are marketing in a multilingual community. Some names have an intense sound (Coca-Cola), others are soft (National). You can use part of your own name, shorten it and attach it to other endings.

In my case, I wanted an 'or' ending. "Secor" can be pronounced just as easily in English as in French or Spanish.

In order to find the name you're looking for, write down all of the possibilities you're considering on a sheet of paper. Get rid of the ones you don't like and keep your ten favourites. Ask your friends next and cross off the ones you don't like. You'll soon find out what your choice should be. Once again, your name is going to be the banner under which you go out and wage battle. So take your time and make sure it feels right for you.

Just imagine a fellow who's over six feet tall, weighs 250 pounds and is known as Mr Little. Some of us might smirk, meeting a man with a name that's in such sharp contrast to his appearance. But Mr Little inherited his name; he didn't have a choice about it.

A business directory may help you in your search for names. For example, the one you're thinking of might already be in use, registered or incorporated. You should have several on hand, just in case. You can also work under your own name. After all, a name like "The Paul Johnson Company" doesn't sound too bad. Your search may take several days unless you've been holding onto a company name for some time already.

Registration or incorporation

In my case, I started operating under a registered company name. This meant that I was personally liable for any of the debts incurred by my various operations.

However, since my income was greater than my expenses, I had a pretty good safety margin.

You can get incorporated for about $300 if you do all the paperwork yourself. A lawyer will ask about $1,000 to do it for you. Incorporation clears you of personal liability for financial obligations taken on by your company.

This structure provides privileges and imposes obligations, such as regularly submitting statements to the government.

At the beginning of my direct marketing operation, I was satisfied simply with registering my company name. I decided to wait until rapid growth would bring me to the incorporation stage. I decided to let my earnings reach a certain level before investing in incorporation. You can certainly do the same.

Skipping a few steps here and there is okay, but don't go off the deep end in your haste to get going.

A distinctive logo

Your logo is your trademark. It identifies your operation. Marlboro sells cigarettes, but what people are really buying is the name. The same principle applies to Dior, Cardin, Lanvin, Mercedes and Coke.

I spent more money on my logo than on my furnishings. My customers can relate to my logo. It's a symbol and carries almost religious weight with them. It's a sign of recognition. It precedes your success in business and provides reassurance. People know they're dealing with the right company when they do business with you. The logo is your trademark and you trademark must inspire confidence. In business, confidence can't be bought, it must be earned.

So go and ask a graphic artist to design your logo. But wait until your business is doing well. It's not imperative to do this right from the start.

What sign will you do business under?

You could always have your mail sent to an anonymous post office box, but this isn't very reassuring for your customers. Do business out in the open. If you want people to believe in you, don't hide from them.

Stationery: heavy artillery for your operations

Never believe for an instant that your letterhead and business cards are only of minimal importance. They are market penetration tools. You will be judged by the visual impact your stationery makes. Packaging and business cards are also extremely important in the business.

The type of paper, its colour, its weight and the accompanying envelope, plus the layout of a (concise!) letter are also keys to success.

I did everything possible so that my stationery and business cards would serve as *customised tools*. Quality counts.

Believe in your idea, and you'll succeed at it

A company, whatever its size, is not created on impulse. Things must be carefully planned. Various errors will be corrected along the way, but the initial plan is always the driving force behind the idea.

How to keep yourself on target:

- Examine established models.
- Read and analyse ads from other direct marketing firms. Examine the other kinds of products that have already been marketed to help you select your product or service (examples are provided at the end of the book).
- Stray from the beaten path. Sell something unusual.
- Provide short- and long-term plans of action.
- Profit from the experience of others. Even though you're trying to innovate, don't be afraid of copying. The Japanese copy, so why not you?

Marketing is big business. The fact that it is so popular in many western countries is the reason why *it's the only profession which you can exercise with a good chance of getting rich fast.*

I devote 10 hours a week to this work at the rate of 2 hours a day.

My system is so fine-tuned that I spend even less time working than I plan and devote more to my favourite pastimes.

You're starting a business. Don't do it halfway. Every detail counts.

CHAPTER 5
HOW TO GET STARTED WITHOUT A PENNY

Once you decide to start your business, you may money where the money is going to come from. If you lack the cash on hand, there are still several other options:

1) A small bank loan

2) A loan from some friends

3) A garage sale to get together the initial capital

4) Plus, a few other alternatives ...

A garage sale might help you bring in some cash, but the first two options will let you get started without laying out a penny of your own – by using other people's money.

Another excellent possibility is obtaining various products from a supplier which are payable in 60 days. This method will give you adequate time to pay back the amounts owed.

Invest in the classifieds

This isn't a new method, but it's an effective one. And classified ads only have to be paid for 30 days after they appear.

By paying your ads after 30 days and your supplier after 60 days, you'll have gotten started without dishing out one red cent.

The bank loan

A small loan from the bank or a personal friend will allow you to pay for operating expenses, stamps, envelopes, etc. – without spending a penny. You still haven't had to dig your hands in your pockets.

Partnerships

Another way to start up inexpensively is to do it together with others. You'll cut your profits, but you'll also bring down the initial investment and risks. Once business is rolling along, you can always drop out of the partnership and go it alone.

Immediate profits

Direct marketing allows you to earn more money almost immediately. Customer response is fast. They'll usually contact you within a few days of placing your ad. The money is there. You're in business.

Easy and profitable

I've been successful in direct marketing, and I feel it's my responsibility to share my success with others, since my method has proved itself.

Proved how easy it is to get rich quick through direct marketing.

The key idea

The key idea, as I've said, is the idea on which everything else is based. You've got to find it and believe in it to the point where you're convinced you're sitting on a pot of gold.

Try it! Perhaps you're a future millionaire who, like me, has a good feel for the subtleties of direct marketing.

CHAPTER 6
SELECTING THE RIGHT PRODUCT

There are many different ways to get free advertising. Some newspaper columnists and radio broadcasters will give plugs to individuals and companies.

Write a brief, interesting story on your product and send it to a reporter or broadcaster. There's a real chance they'll do a report on it.

If you don't have an exclusive product when you start out, you can sell a service. We live in a time when services are highly valued. I have a friend who sold résumés through the mail. Another offers language courses which he's prepared himself. It goes without saying that he knows his languages well. And a Hispanic friend lives quite well by teaching a correspondence course which allows his students to become proficient in Spanish in one month. Self-improvement courses also are one of the vast range of services which sell well.

When I started out in this prosperous direct marketing industry, I spent a good deal of time seeking out the right products to sell through the mail.

I'm an expert fisherman, and there are millions of fishing fanatics in the area where I live. So, I started off by serving an obvious market which I know well.

The question was, what to sell?

- Fancy bait?
- Some new-fangled knife?
- A fish detector?

After giving the problem a bit of thought, I finally opted for a safety line in a nylon pouch. This is an indispensable precaution on a boat. Its main feature is that you can hold the pouch in one hand, hurl it forwards and let the line spin out automatically for 60 feet.

I had managed to get hold of an almost exclusive item which served a target group concerned with its safety.

This example simply shows how you can fill a sometimes very specific need, as I successfully did with my safety line.

In his book, *The Lazy Man's Way to Riches*, J. Karbo, an American businessman, lists a number of approaches which can be applied with only a little imagination. Everything from weight-loss plans to jump ropes can be sold through direct marketing.

Bookstores and publishers

Direct marketing is a considerable source of profit for North American publishers. Many bookstores make major *mailings* of numerous titles. Certain organisations have lists of millions of names and some individuals have lists with more than a million names.

The direct marketing industry is experiencing incredible growth. It is the field of the future and I quickly understood, as you shall too, that the networking factor is a source of enormous profit. Each time the post office delivers a dozen sacks stuffed with letters and money orders for specific items, it strikes home how there's no other way to make so much money in so little time. Because ad response is very quick (from within a few days to 2 or 3 weeks), you know right away if your product will, or won't, sell.

What can you sell by direct marketing?

Here are a few of the classic items:

- Clothing
- Office equipment (small items)
- Kitchen equipment
- Photographic equipment
- Jewellery
- Pet food
- Plants
- Small electronic devices
- Books
- Health-care products
- Records
- Gadgets, gizmos, etc.
- Good-luck charms
- Miraculous objects

You can make this list as long as you want:

- Marriage counselling
- Real-estate advice
- Recreational tips: fishing, hunting, camping
- Carpentry skills (for the hobbyist)
- Water-sports advice
- Advertising techniques

Services can extend to an incredible number of subjects:

- Astrology
- Translation
- Advertising
- Public relations and even direct marketing

One of my buddies, Ray Fern, has had amazing results with imports. He had the funds to let him purchase stocks of jewellery and exotic items from Egypt which were not available elsewhere.

Then there's loofah. You may be asking yourself what's a loofah. It's a vegetable sponge which, when cleaned, can be used as a household sponge. Middle Easterners have been using this plant, with its skin-restorative powers, for thousands of years. Once its seeds have been removed, this sponge can be used for a multitude of purposes, ranging from skin care to household chores, like washing dishes.

Ray stumbled on to a gold mine. The item costs little, weighs little and responds to a need.

The ideal object

If you decide on shipping through the mail, eliminate objects which are heavy, difficult to package, costly to send, or too fragile.

The description

You'll be describing your product in minute detail in your brochure. Don't forget anything. You want your customer to know what he's getting. In my case, outside of the detailed description of the article I want to sell, I include pictures as well as very detailed illustrations. I use an artist who faithfully reproduces the object.

For example: We arc selling a plastic ruler including inches, picas, agate lines, metric system and centigrade conversions, printing measurements, grid, screen angle selection and different fonts, etc. for $9.95.

This exclusive product is made to order and is essential for all printing applications.

The description of this plastic ruler is complete. It lets the customer know what he's getting. The more detail you give him, the more likely he is to buy from you.

So make sure you give the customer a thorough description. Don't omit any relevant information on the item you want to sell.

Need

A few key factors will help determine which product you should select:

a) Need for the product

b) Type of product

c) A high demand for this product

d) Quality

e) Ease of shipping

Shipping delays will cut down on profits. The item ordered must be sent immediately. If you want your customers to be happy, keep some stock on hand.

Motivation

Why has direct marketing experienced such phenomenal success? We'll answer this question by asking another one. Why has the Catholic Church been able to preside over such a huge congregation for centuries and impose its dictates on it?

The Church advises that everyone, rich or poor, is guilty of the seven capital sins. Theologians made sure that they defined a territory which included all human beings. Within the hierarchy of sins, there are two classes: big and small. Some sins don't matter that much, while others are mortal. The seven capital sins are part of a Christian ideology which inherited the concept primarily from Judaism.

Thus, similar forces have driven people over the centuries:

Gluttony: Immoderate eating and drinking. This sin, not always such a cute one, has generated a giant sweets industry. We shall spare ourselves from considering this subject *ad nauseam*. It is enough to mention that excessive eating has given rise to a vast number of health-care industries preaching moderation. And specialists combat obesity with lots of advertising hubbub on the obvious effects of gluttony.

Pride: Pride not only involves the excessive love of one's self. It also turns a person into a first-class copycat. It makes him go out and get a car as big as his neighbour's. Pride often goes hand-in-hand with envy – a predisposition to vanity.

Pleasures of the Flesh: What can't be sold to satisfy the pleasures of the flesh? Certain kinds of magazines make a fortune. An entire industry has been born out of the appetite for erotic books, videos, etc.

Without giving a treatise here on religious morality, it can safely be said that human impulses govern the human condition. It's possible to change events, but you won't alter man's basic nature.

The exclusive product

Finding an exclusive product will make it easier to make money through direct marketing. This eliminates competition. However, it's not always easy to find such a product, unless you have it made for yourself. This requires extending the range of your business and entails considerable investment.

Anyone who looks around a little will find many interesting and exclusive products. The government publishes catalogues which cover all the products made in a particular region and also include craftsmen with whom you can make deals to help move one or more of the products they make.

Characteristics of products which sell well

The following list of products is far from exhaustive. But these products always have, and always will be, very successful in direct marketing.

- Glassware
- Gifts
- Gloves
- Food
- Exercise equipment
- Binoculars
- Books
- Telephone equipment
- Correspondence courses
- Magnifying glasses
- Decorative objects
- Clocks/watches
- Tools
- Spices
- Medallions
- Collector's Items
- Shoes
- Health-care products
- Paints
- Lamps
- Figurines
- Souvenirs
- Beauty items
- Games (magic tricks)
- Fishing equipment
- Etchings
- Pens
- Plant products (all types of seeds)

This list can go on practically forever. Other examples are included at the end of the book.

Information of all kinds

- Cassettes
- Magazines
- Letters
- Data Banks
- Manuals
- Books
- Newspapers
- Advice
- Photos
- Different types of methods

Keeping track of ideas

Memory is not perfect. I write everything down so I don't forget anything. When I get an idea, I put it on paper. I don't always use it immediately, but experience has shown that I lose nothing this way and the information will always be available when the right moment presents itself.

Personally, I like to sell information.

If you want to invest in producing a book, it is essential, as you will see further on, to carefully plan your idea. In order not to get stuck, keep some room to manoeuvre. In a print shop, a machine can break down or the workers can go on strike. You're not responsible for imponderables, but they do exist.

Good planning avoids many costly mistakes.

CHAPTER 7
WHO WILL YOUR CUSTOMERS BE?

At the beginning of my career in direct marketing, I was worried that I would have trouble finding customers. I started by doing research on potential competitors. They existed, but where did they advertise? As part of my research, I read all available tabloids and popular magazines for a week.

I carefully maintained a *file* on each of my competitors, calculated the space they purchased, studied their solicitation methods and noted the keys to their success. Sometimes they published their ads on specific days. I was finally ready for my own test.

Classified ads

I was divided as to whether I should:

1) Purchase a large advertising space

   or

2) Use small inserts to test my products

   I finally opted for classifieds in different publications. Before making any large-scale *investments*, which I would do later for specific products, I needed to comprehensively understand how advertising investment worked.

   The *classifieds* provided a good way of getting products moving. They don't cost a lot, but they deliver. In addition, since you're billed at a future date, you can immediately capitalise on your earnings and pay later. And even if you place a lot of ads, they won't ruin you, as the amount you'll have to pay is almost always very small compared with your earnings.

   Once you've put together a certain amount of capital, you'll be able to invest in bigger ads, by purchasing space proportional to your earnings.

   I think that anyone getting started in direct marketing should proceed step by step. Getting to know your market well and dealing with its subtleties requires time.

   My classifieds put me in touch with ten customers – first nibbles for what would turn out to be a whale of a business.

Advertising: the stakes

If you're going to be doing a lot of advertising, you can negotiate lower rates. The cost of a line of text in a daily paper decreases according to volume. A large department store won't pay the same for a full page ad as an individual who advertises only occasionally. Negotiate. Your regular appearance in a publication will help you save lots of money because of volume. So don't invest blindly.

The message

Write concisely. Make each word count. Work on it. You must create a need. Emphasise various key words by underlining them. Use different kinds of characters, screens and white on black lettering. My own tactic is to get testimonials.

For example:

With Senecol ... I got back that great-to -be -alive feeling

Health-care products benefit from this approach. Personal testimonials reassure and generate confidence.

Whenever possible, attach a coupon to the ad and give a phone number. Filling out a coupon requires a certain amount of effort and mobilises the customer's resources. He has to concentrate. The telephone lets you reach out to your customers. It's cold and anonymous, but works fast, particularly when buying on impulse. By giving your customer a coupon and phone number, he has two ways to buy from you, not just one. Nonetheless, the coupon is *vital* and indispensable for encouraging a return.

Psychology of the potential customer

Big companies understand the value of including return envelopes with a bill. Do you think these companies spend so much just on glamour? Hardly. Their experience has shown that most customers aren't in any hurry to send a cheque. A small, personalised envelope usually gets them moving. The envelope is an exception to the daily routine. More than a reminder, it is an obligation.

In order to work well, your *message* should include the following key elements:

- An address
- A phone number
- A coupon

On a few occasions, I was unfortunate enough to forget to include either the phone number or coupon. The results were disappointing.

Trial offers

Trial offers can help you prospect a territory. Guarantees are a must.

It is understood that I can return this book if I am not satisfied.

Specify:

Within ten days following receipt ... however this notice can be deferred and extended over several weeks.

Very few people return a book within the time provided. Because of other obligations, they forget, until they're reminded by the bill. Big companies (such as *Time-Life*) count on a recipient's inertia. The return rate is insignificant.

Where to place your ad

Most publications ask 10% more for a pre-determined position. I always like my ads to be on the right-hand side of the page. Readers usually look to the right when they open a newspaper or magazine.

Nonetheless, if you don't get a right-hand spot, don't panic. Put your ad on a well-read page. The advertising department should be able to give you statistics on this.

In addition to the main ad, I'll place three or four *teasers* in the publication, to help motivate customers.

Select the right time period

Don't just place your ads any old time. There are key days. Big department stores like Wednesdays and Thursdays, to stimulate weekend sales. Advertising on holidays is bad practice. You're throwing your money away. Avoid school vacations, election campaigns and strikes. Although the latter may be unpredictable, the union usually gives advance warning.

The worst months for advertising are December, June, July and August. Newspapers are also subject to seasonal trends.

The right media

What do you mean when you say "the right media"? In the case of direct marketing, this probably won't be a high-circulation, intellectually oriented vehicle.

The right media has mass appeal and meets the following criteria:

- High circulation
- Attractive cover
- Visually appealing contents
- Catchy titles
- A specific market
- Solid new stand distribution. The more outlets where it can be purchased, the better you'll do.

Such newspapers and magazines exist. *Selecting* the right ones depends to a large measure on the products you want to move. If they are household items, put your ad in a women's magazine. If it's for office equipment, business magazines are excellent vehicles.

Financing and paying for your ad

If you're not well-known, the various media are not likely to give you credit, unless you can come up with solid guarantees. You'll be asked either for cash up front, or payment in two instalments:

1) the first when you sign for the ad

2) the rest when the proofs are delivered

Don't be put off by the attitude of the advertising department. They've seen it all, and, based on their previous experiences, don't want to get stuck with a bad deal. Don't count on getting large ads on credit.

Address lists

There are some good companies which lease address lists. Such addresses obviously don't "belong" to you. The list that you compile will be based on the responses you receive.

These organisations don't give you addresses. You simply bring them envelopes and they mail them for you.

You might launch an operation by leasing 7-8,000 addresses. Later on, when the money comes in, make up your own address file.

PCs will also allow you to set up a large, up-to-date file.

Respect postal regulations

Learn about the post office regulations with which you must comply. Whether you're using postal or sealed envelopes, you've got to know what a large-scale mailing will cost.

The brochure

Visually catching, it should *illustrate* everything that a letter might contain. In other words, it must be attractive and make people want to look at it.

The order form

The more clear and concise it is, the easier it will be to fill out. Don't try to produce complicated forms with a pompous style. The key *idea* is what should convince your clients.

The return envelope

If big businesses do it, why not you? Your prospective clients don't want to go to any trouble to order from you. Spare them the grief of having to look for an envelope and write your company's name and address on it. Make the job easy for them.

Personalised letter

If you solicit with a personalised letter, don't typeset it. Type it, then print it. Use a classic type face with a nice layout.

Here is a typical example:

February 4, 1987

Dear friend,

Do you want to succeed?

Would you like to fully enjoy life, travel, and do all this while your bank account gets bigger and bigger?

We have a job for you.

How would you like to be our representative without leaving your present occupation? Our proposal is simple.

(Get right into the subject. Without being heavy, get to the point).

Have you ever dreamed of going into business for yourself? This is the opportunity you've been waiting for!

(Your letter should be friendly and no longer than one page. However, in some cases, the length of the letter is not, in and of itself, terribly important).

We are available to provide you with all the information you'll need to make a quick decision. Your success is our success.

(Include your address and phone number)

I include my business card with such letters. It's printed on vellum paper, has a sober colour and contains the essentials. Plus a phone number and the note: "Personal and confidential".

The imagination to the rescue

There are hundreds of techniques of persuasion. Some are more subtle than others. How well it will work depends on how good your imagination is. A great imagination can leap over great hurdles. List the elements which will contribute to your success. Plus, always keep your eyes open for new ways of doing things and original methods.

Don't be afraid to be daring.

At a time when puritan attitudes were still prevalent, I was one of the first to sell erotic materials by direct marketing. One of my letters began:

Come here you little devil!

You can guess the rest. Within record time, I'd moved 50,000 copies of a small book on the world's 100 best positions for making love.

CHAPTER 8
GIVE YOUR ADS THAT EXTRA ZING

One of my friends, a marketing executive, keeps a series of key buzz words on hand which invariably recur periodically in his advertising texts.

We might give some consideration to this aspect of sales. I separate it into three headings;

- *The product*
- *Motivation*
- *Persuasion*

The product

I have never sold a product without knowing it well, as though it needed to be part of me. If I don't know it well at the start, I get information on it. I read everything there is that was ever written on the subject.

In order to be *highly successful* in sales, you have to prepare yourself for whatever might happen through an in-depth knowledge of the product, which may often be distributed through various avenues or outlets.

Motivation

We know what makes people act:

- Envy
- Desire to own
- Wanting to be prominent
- Money
- Sex
- Security
- Trendiness

Sex and money

These two go hand-in-hand. Haven't you ever heard that you don't get one with the other? Whether or not this is true, these are two powerful motivational tools which can make businesses flourish (Playboy, Penthouse) and which also support thousands of private clubs where money buys the pleasures of sex. Just consider pornography and related industries and the successful businessmen who live off human desires.

When I started my business, I said to myself (as perhaps you've said to yourself):

"you can't change the world." There is nothing I can do about it and if I wanted to launch some kind of a crusade, my own little voice would be lost among the masses.

So, if you want to learn about money and you want to accumulate some, act accordingly and be profit oriented. The merchants and businessmen of the world operate according to the *needs* of others. Such needs exist and it's up to you to try to fulfil them in your own way. This doesn't prevent you from being honest, however. You should always be honest with your customers.

In the previous chapter, we discussed advertising material and copy and the role that these elements will play to create the best possible impression of you and your product.

The emphasis

Look at various ads. Marlboro puts its emphasis on cowboys and wild horses, rather than the cigarettes themselves. They convey a message of virility.

There is a series of tricks of the trade that you can use. And the emphasis is to *hook* the customer, hold onto him and totally fascinate him for a brief moment.

The ritual

All messages should have an almost mystical element which is part of an "initiation" into the use of the product. As if you were participating in a ritual. A sublime rite. You may think this isn't professional, but anyone who's good at sales has the ability to once in a while to blow his customer away with a few key phrases which pack a real wallop.

Key selling words

The list is long, so I'll cite a few examples here:

– Unique	– Exclusive
– Free	– Secret
– Seductive	– Dream
– Spectacular	– You
– New	

Dictionaries of antonyms and synonyms can provide you with quite a long list. Clip out ads which grab your imagination. I do this regularly, and the practice has proven valuable on more than one occasion. There is much to be learned from others, and even more since marketing techniques are evolving at such a rapid rate. Put on your thinking cap! Let it go to work. And use your friends as a *think tank*.

How: the magic word

Even if it's been used a lot, it still hasn't lost its touch:

How I managed to lose 20 pounds in 1 month the easy way.

How invites the reader to take part in a ritual. It testifies to personal experience.

How to get rich using other people's money.

How implies there's a magic formula. *It reveals a secret.* It invites the customer/reader to experiment with a way to achieve personal success.

If there was no *how*, the concept would certainly have to be invented. But it exists. So use it! Its value is well established.

The text which sells

It is short, snappy and convincing

- Gives a good picture of the object
- Makes it fascinating
- Is exclusive
- Is musical
- Has a nice ring
- Is uplifting

It hooks you

The text speaks. As a writer once said, don't take *words* lightly. Words can trigger a divorce or even unleash a war.

The first draft

After you write a piece of copy you like, let it sit around for a few days, unless you're under pressure to move faster. But why be under such pressure? You're spending money for an expensive ad and you should give yourself the chance to fully evaluate it beforehand. You're only doing yourself a favour.

The second draft

Improve the first draft by changing a word here, a sentence there. Ask a friend to read it. What doesn't feel right? Your friend's reactions will probably cause you to make additional changes. The text should be fine-tuned until it hums along perfectly.

My method: paste it up

I start by writing out my text in full. Once I've done this, I break it up into small blocks. I place the different elements of my ad on a large white sheet of paper, like I'm putting together a jigsaw puzzle. This lets me see the special effects of my ad, the catch lines and the visual layout.

A photocopying machine is particularly useful for this layout, because I can reduce or enlarge titles and pictures.

When it all seems right, I make a copy of the layout and keep correcting it until it's perfect.

This gives me a fast and solid overview of the visual impact.

Next, I typeset the ad, to make sure I will get exactly what I want. This protects me from any unpleasant surprises, since so many unforseeable mistakes can crop up in ad production.

Are you sceptical?

Reading all this, you're probably telling yourself: "It's too good to be true!"

I was also sceptical at the beginning.

But, after a few weeks, almost all the apparent obstacles vanished.

Get to work.

What's difficult is not the work awaiting you, rather, it's your *willingness* to *undertake a new career* which can *bring in* big bucks.

I could offer you a heap of wise, tested advice, but it's not up to me to make up your mind for *you*.

Use of illustrations in your ads

They say a picture's worth a thousand words. Most people look at pictures before reading text.

The caption accompanying the picture should seal the deal. It should be as convincing as the picture itself.

Very long texts

They've got to have real impact and must be written convincingly. They normally have more *impact* than short texts, which sometimes leave the reader hanging.

North American ads often rely on extensive copy. Copywriters are able to muster up a whole kaleidoscope of convincing arguments.

Words to avoid

Don't use *I*, *me*, *myself*. There's nothing worse than constant repetition of *me*, *me*, *me*. Anyone starting off with *I* loses a lot of credibility.

- *I* did this
- In that instance, *I* knew in advance
- *I* have enough of
- *I* said it. *I* predicted it.

Spiking the text with *I*'s and *me*'s is pointless, unless they conjure up a forceful, motivating personality for the reader. The repeated use of *I* or *me* is particularly exasperating because it fails to convince. Stay away from these words like the plague and use the following ones instead:

– *Our* mutual project
– *Our* hopes are the same
– *You* have the necessary qualities
– *Your* problems really aren't problems.
– *We* have things in common.

Your reader or listener is not concerned with your states of being.

He is concerned with *himself*.

Talk to him about his problems, not yours.

Get interested in *his life*. Your own does nothing for him.

There is one exception to this rule: *product endorsements*.

If sincerity rings loud and clear from your text, the reader will identify with the word *me*. He'll say: "This guy is just like *me!*"

When using *I* in a testimonial, the text should be solidly constructed in order to work well.

"I've suffered from chronic constipation for four years"

Identification factor: millions of people, especially women, suffer from chronic constipation.

In this case, the *I* takes on a positive value.

I felt worn out, depressed, weak, unable to do my work well. Some days, *I* hardly wanted to go on living.

In today's world, this kind of depression is experienced by millions of people. *You* are speaking on behalf of the chronically depressed, who are looking for a way out of their problems. The *I* becomes representative: people can identify with it and relate to it.

Preachers don't tell their congregations that: "I want to save my soul". Rather, they bring the faithful together by urging, "If we want, we can save our souls."

So put the *I* where it will have impact value: in the testimonial.

Don't be too smart for your own good

When I started out, I had the tendency to intellectualise my ad copy. Don't make the same mistake. If you mention famous people in your copy, use the following sort of reference:

George Washington used to talk about the need to see big. You must see big in order to accomplish anything.

People like to identify with someone well known and respected. Using quotes from such people is an excellent strategy.

Continuity

If you successfully market a product, make sure you can keep it going. Each product must be followed by another. Maintain a list of item you want to sell.

Coupons

You should be sure to leave enough space in reply coupons so that your customer won't have to scribble his address as an illegible mess. The new name should be added to your mailing list. So remember to leave that space.

Name _____

Address_____

Post code or Zip code (US) _____

The need to save space might make you consider cutting the size of that coupon. But before you do, put yourself in the shoes of the customer who wants to subscribe to your offer – if only you make it easy enough for him to do so.

Your success depends on your ability to guess his needs without him having to go to the trouble of dealing with your oversights.

CHAPTER 9
HOW THE BUYER THINKS

Who are your customers?

What do they want from you?

There's a simple answer to both questions.

We live in an era of intensive communication, but at the same time, there's never been so much loneliness. Couples split up after a few years together and find themselves alone, and not too anxious to be hurt all over again. Alimony takes a portion of divorced men's income, and many wish to remain single and get more involved with their own lives.

Men and women today are two worlds apart.

A communications link

It took me little time to understand that I *was acting* like a communications link between two emotional poles. My customers will probably be yours as well. Direct marketing has not only a practical dimension, but a psychological one as well.

I wanted to support a basic theory I had, so I surveyed several hundred people from various backgrounds.

Here are some of the things they said:

Gigi S.   I prefer mail order for several reasons: if I like an item, I buy it. I get into the process of receiving and opening a package.

Carl B.   This is how I maintain ongoing communication with the outside world. Outside of my work, which doesn't do much for me, my social life is limited. I'm on the lookout for interesting offers and I spend several hundred dollars on mail order items each year.

Eddy T.   It's sort of like a hobby or a game. If there's a catch, I lose interest right away.

Elizabeth T. It's a bit like buying a lottery ticket for me. In a lottery, if you don't win, nothing happens. With mail order, at least you're sure of getting something.

Malcolm H.   People get into certain things. Myself, I love surprises. I order products on impulse. I want to be able to see and feel what I've ordered. I always hope that I haven't been fooled.

The *expectation* factor was a consistently strong motivating force among all of the people questioned.

They were *waiting* for something to happen.

"When you're by yourself, leading a dreary life, with nothing except and armchair and a paper, you have to do something to forget your loneliness," explains Christine M., a 32 year-old nurse, who has enough money to buy whatever she fancies. She doesn't like crowds or going out and buys all of her books through the mail.

Ginny B.   I'm always on the lookout for all kinds of things I can get by mail order, depending on what I need at a given moment. I sometimes treat myself to cosmetics, my weak spot. I also like books, and there are always plenty of interesting ones to choose from.

A trusting environment

You've decided to start your own business? Congratulations. Give yourself a few days to decide which product you're going to sell. Knowing how to choose is a guarantee of success. Once you have this product, provide good service to your customers. Integrity counts.

Your customers will stay with you if you know how to *sustain* their needs, interest and curiosity by proposing several articles, one after the other, rather than just one item and one alone. You must maintain your customers' interest. You can't take it for granted that they're yours for life.

From dreams to reality

Direct marketing, in its own way, puts dreams up for sale. By cutting out the middlemen, you establish a close interaction with your customers.

If you're late in delivering, you'll be overloaded with telephone calls like this:

"You told me I'd get it in four days ..."

"I sent you a money order and I want to know what's going on. Did you forget about me?"

People will write to you as well. Expect to get annoying letters if you fail to fulfil all of the conditions of the agreement.

Because an agreement – or even more important, a contract based on gut feelings – is involved.

You can't mess around.

Once, even twice, you can trick your customer. But you'll lose him forever if you fail to fulfil his expectations.

He is ready to pay. He can understand that you've got your own break-in problems because of unforseeables you've got to deal with.

But he won't stand for you letting him down.

The customer's always right

If you want to know to what extent you can trust your future customers, I'd assure you that they're not out to rip you off. They're responsible people. Their cheques (if that's what they send) are good.

Here and there, in a big volume business, you may occasionally run into a problem or two. But it's rare.

Direct marketing proved itself in North America a long time ago.

You are joining a club with its own membership rules. They are well-established rules and neither customers nor suppliers have any interest in cheating each other.

Chapter 10
How to work with your printers

As a specialist in direct marketing, you should have various printers available to do your work: form letters, circulars, envelopes, different kinds of brochures, books, etc.

It may take you a little time to find the right printer – one who'll work fast at a reasonable price.

Large operations

These kinds of operations are loaded with back orders and thus not likely to offer you any *price breaks*. No more likely than you'll get those 20,000 letters printed overnight.

Large printers set up their schedules a long time in advance and are organised around computers. Their volume is enormous, and a silly little order of 20,000 letters is not going to impress them and change their proven planning methods.

Smaller printers

Head for medium-size operations. They'll probably work all night to fill an order and keep you happy.

Bids

In order to avoid unpleasant surprises, ask for bids. Before ordering anything, you should know exactly what it will cost. Insist on the following three criteria:

• Quality

• Meeting the deadline

• Firm price

Let the least expensive bid win.

A perfect text

Save money by taking your carefully prepared copy to the typesetter.

Texts should be double-spaced on A4-sized paper to facilitate correction. Have you ever tried correcting single-spaced text? The job is twice as tough.

Clarity, precision and layout are *keys to your success*. Don't forget them.

If you give the typesetter a barely legible draft, expect a big bill, since his work will take twice as long as it would have with neater copy.

The layout

Once you've decided to print a brochure, make sure that the typesetter receives a layout in which all of the different elements – text, pictures and titles – clearly appear. It shouldn't be too rough. Don't present an incomplete job which you'll fiddle around with as the spirit so moves you.

The typeface

Most well organised printers will be able to show you a catalogue of the different typefaces in stock: Gothic, Helvetica, Times, etc. Type sizes are also indicated (6, 8, 10, 12, 14, etc). Figuring out size and face is so easy a child could do it. Even if you aren't up on the fine points of how a print shop is organised, you can still get your job done right. Plus, the printer can give you advice.

I make sure I get my job done the way I want by first getting it typeset and then taking it to the printer.

There are two distinct operations involved. Either you let the printer do everything (typesetting and printing) or you split up the two steps involved in producing the brochure.

At the beginning, it's better to let the printer handle everything and avoid a lot of footwork. But make sure you understand that typesetters set type and don't print. And many printers don't set type – they just print.

If you decide to print an exclusive book

By this stage, your business should be going well. You've got a good *idea*, and you are almost certain that your customers would like an *exclusive book*.

This is much more complicated than ordering 10,000 envelopes or a simple brochure.

How to proceed

If you're not a great writer, you can order the job from a *ghost writer*. This is a professional writer who works on contract. You assign a *subject* and you both sign an agreement on his fee.

Prices vary according to the value of the job and the number of pages. Expect to pay between $2,500 and $3,000 for a 200-page book. Prices vary according to the subject. A specialised book requires more time and attention. Some companies make it their business to write for other companies. There are so few of these, you can count them all on the fingers of one hand. For a set fee, they'll produce a work from "A to Z" and deliver the finished product to you. Obviously, you will call upon specialists when your business allows it and when you have the resources to invest in an exclusive product.

Different stages

Once the ghost-writer has completed the manuscript and you've accepted it, you'll get it typeset. This part of the job should take around six days.

Checking the proofs

The typesetter will give you proofs to be corrected. If you need to make any changes, this will be your last chance to do so.

The layout

You know how you want the book to look. In your preliminary layout, you should indicate to the typesetter:

a) The appearance of chapter headings

b) The selection of typefaces

c) The location of any pictures or illustrations

This information will make it easy for a paste-up artist to produce the final layout according to the model you provide.

Covers

Plan and prepare your covers in advance so that you can start your print run as soon as possible after receiving the proofs. Printing the covers is an independent operation. Since the cover is the book's package, it should look right and the work should be done by an illustrator.

The cost will run from about $300 to $500, depending on the type of cover and the illustrator you choose.

The visual appearance

As the distributors of several exclusive editions, I always take great care in how a book is packaged. It must be striking. Even the best book will sell poorly with a so-so, hastily thrown together cover.

The example below will allow you to draw your own conclusions.

One day, in a grocery store, I stopped to observe the customers. There was a large selection of dried fruits, dates, figs, raisins and prunes on the counter. In one large jar there were some fairly lifeless looking prunes, and in the other, some shiny ones. Why were they different? I noticed that the customers tended to prefer the good-looking prunes. I imagined there was a reason for the difference, so I asked the merchant what it was.

"It's very simple," he said. "Here you have untreated, natural prunes and over there you have prunes soaked in glucose. That's what gives them their vital appearance. Customers like what shines."

He obviously sold twice as many glucosed prunes as natural, dull ones.

Although clothes might not make the man, packaging a product is the key to selling it.

Don't be afraid to spend whatever you have to for packaging. Remember: our world is a visual one.

The details

You'll quickly get the hang of it. You'll learn while doing. Let your printer take care of folding, stapling, glueing and cutting. That's his job.

There are also a certain number of key items you should understand so that you'll become acquainted with the technical side of printing. They consist of a limited number of reference points such as:

CAP	for capital letters
LC	for lower case letter
BW	Black and white
Screen	Shades (10, 20, 30, 40, etc.)
Inverses –	white on black lettering
Titles and captions	above and below pictures or drawings
Rules	thin lines. There is a whole set of them.

Your printer is a partner in your success. The quality of your advertising material will be your trademark.

Chapter 11
Your number 1 partner

You have a number 1 partner.

Before going further in your new business, contact it.

It's the post office, without which there wouldn't be any direct marketing.

A sympathetic ear

The postal system counts on you to boost its volume so they can achieve a profitable level of operation.

Back when I got started, I gave my postal representative a call:

> "Hello."

> "Hello. I'm soon planning on using the postal system as part of my business."

> "That's good news for us. Do you have any idea of how much you'll be sending each week or month?"

> "About 20,000 circulars per week."

Before I could say another word, the rep offered to send me an expert who could answer all my questions.

By noon, I knew everything I wanted to know on how to deal with the intricacies of the postal system, and had a pile of documents to explain the details. Like most people, I hadn't known there was so much material available.

The *post office* is a business. It is geared to making a profit and its representatives have every reason to treat you with respect and help you.

The system and your product

Once the post office knows what you plan to send, it will let you know how to do your mailing, prepare your packages, provide your postage, what your costs will be, how to arrange your shipments, and what special rates, rights and obligations you have.

Don't get exasperated. Everything is arranged so that you can be served efficiently.

Even if you spend an incredible amount on some other type of shipment, it will never be as efficient as the post office. The post office has resources that other shippers don't have. Its staff, trucks, electronic equipment, networks and routes are at your disposal. The money you pay the post office will be quickly transformed into profits.

We'll say it once more. Without the post office, you will not be able to start up your direct marketing business.

In order to save time

You should talk with the post office about mass-mailing circulars or any problems you might have in sending packages. You'll save time and money by putting this very willing giant to work for you.

Packages

You have to take a few basic precautions before sending some items through the mail. Packages get banged around a lot. Items must be properly packaged. Many companies make all kinds of solid, padded, rugged envelopes in different sizes which can withstand a bit of abuse.

I'm not going to recommend one company over another, but you can easily find suppliers of these products in the *Yellow Pages*.

Stamps

If you make massive mailings and your envelopes bear return addresses, the post office will assign you a bulk rate number which eliminates the need to purchase stamps.

Or, you can use a postage machine.

Applying postage is made much easier by using such a device.

Postal rate increases

The post office regularly ups its rates. If you stay in touch with your postal representative, he'll advise you in advance of any anticipated price hikes in time for you to respond accordingly.

CHAPTER 12
MANAGING YOUR BUSINESS

All businesses require good management . Whether your company is big or small, you have to know where it's at on a daily basis. Are you making money? Are you losing any? Your system of accounting should be as simple as possible.

Example

Item:	How much I've saved	Day	Year
Number of orders	_____	____	____
Cash received	_____	____	____
Money orders	_____	____	____
Cheques	_____	____	____
Total	_____	____	____
Cash	_____	____	____
Cheques	_____	____	____
Money	_____	____	____
Orders	_____	____	____

OTHER BUSINESS

DESCRIPTION
_____

GENERAL COMMENTS
_____

Total earnings for Thursday, *January 24*

This table is an example, and not necessarily the model to follow.

It's up to you to understand that you have to carefully keep track of everything. You can subsequently draw up a tighter accounting summary, with statistics and by region, for example. You'll be able to quickly establish which products work and which don't.

I like statistics. They help me understand who my customers are, what they expect and what kind of product I can sell them. This involves a more complex, analytically oriented accounting system which is based on facts and figures.

There are excellent regions for conducting tests. If a product works in such a region, it will work elsewhere as well.

Sorting out orders

This will not always be easy. Why? Many of your customers will write illegibly. The money is there, but whom do you send the package to? If your customer has enclosed a cheque, you can always locate him, since he'll get hold of you in a week or two if he's received nothing for his money yet. The main idea is to reassure him so that he doesn't get angry and run off to file a complaint for fraud.

Don't throw anything away

When sorting orders, you may be tempted to throw away some envelope which seems hopelessly lost. *Don't do it.* Put it in a special file called "customer problems". You'll have a few of them if you've received cash. The best thing which could happen under such circumstances is that a customer calls up to complain that he didn't get his order. Don't ignore such problems. Deal with them.

Keep a careful record of all letters you receive. These are also names to add to your list. In a little while, you'll have thousands of names.

If you're organised – and you will be later on – you'll produce an alphabetised computer list.

Have I mentioned what an excellent tool computers are for working with data? They will let you know your state of affairs in practically no time at all.

As your business grows, equip yourself accordingly. You're working to make money, but not kill yourself doing so.

A good accountant

Unless you decide to do everything yourself, which is perhaps necessary at the start, you'd be well advised to retain the services of an accountant who will help you set up an accounting system. The best system will be one that anyone can understand with just a few explanations.

CONCLUSION
HOW TO MULTIPLY YOUR FORTUNE

Are you afraid of someone stealing your customer list? If so, put it in a safety deposit box. Are you afraid of fire and vandalism? If so, take precautions.

List rental

Renters need not be afraid of professional customer-list thieves in North America. One of direct marketing's great experts, and probably the person with the most knowledge in the field, recently explained to me why the risks are so small.

"I often rent lists with 50,000 names (at 2 cents per name) without a hitch. In any event, word travels fast within the industry. There is the occasional rip-off artist, but rental companies know how to protect themselves."

So don't worry about someone pillaging your fortune. You generally know who you're doing business with.

I *rent* my lists and have never had a problem about it.

It's good to protect your fortune, but not to the point to sit tight, in the fear that one of your prospective customers would nick a list.

Anyone can do it

You may have got the impression, reading this book, that setting up a direct marketing firm is quite complicated. Get rid of the illusion. It's easy. Anyone can do it. All that's required is a bit of initiative, a place to work and appealing ideas for products and services.

You should start by looking for one or more interesting products. They can be easily found. If you like books, remember that publishers frequently clear out large stocks. You can buy up unsold lots, which, unfortunately, won't provide you with an exclusive sales territory.

One of my friends had a craftsman make small boxes for artists' materials, easels and other kinds of objects that could only be purchased through him.

Another designed a steak knife rack. It consists of a piece of wood with six openings in which the knife blades fit. Not a bad idea at all, and practical. Your articles must correspond to specific needs.

I make money and have a good time doing it

From the start of my direct marketing operations, my bank account has been sky rocketing. Believe me, nothing is more useful than money!

I remember a meeting I had once in Philadelphia, a few months after I launched my first product. I met a fellow named Joe Harting, one of the most ingenious guys I'd ever encountered.

Joe was really into business. He sold old magazines to collectors. His wife, Mary, would grow through the mail each day. She got upset if there were less than $3000 in orders. Like manna from heaven.

Joe told me that a lot of people toss away old magazines, although they're interesting and contain gold mines of information. "*I sell information*, special issues on specific subjects, and make a fortune," he told me.

Joe had a huge file, including lists of all the American papers. He sorted his subjects according to category:

- Parents
- Warfare
- Electronics
- Space
- Sports

In this way, he created extensive files on various subjects and sold them through direct marketing.

I haven't seen Joe since then, but I imagine by now he's retired, young and rich, out in sunny California.

You can also be a successful businessman – the easy way.

Direct marketing is the key to the future, as well as to success and fortune.

Direct marketing is the way to go, if you don't mind earning big bucks and living well.

REFERENCE LIST A
MAGAZINES WITH IDEAS ON
PRODUCTS TO LAUNCH

You can contact:

Business Opportunities Digest

Britain's top business opportunities newsletter. Mails monthly to its subscribers. The lastest and best news, views and monthly mailing ideas from Britain and around the world. For details write to B.O.D., 28 Charles Square, London N1 6HT

Business Opportunities World-wide Imp.-Exp. Promotion

P.O.B. 503, Marine Parade Post Office
Singapore 15
Republic of Singapore
Export-Gazette
Narang House
K. 1 Ambalal Doshli Marg.
Bombay 400001
India

Foreign Trade Communication

P.O.B. 164
Koba
Japan

Korea Directory

Korean Chamber of Commerce & Industry
111, Sonkong-Dong, Choong-ku
Seoul, Korea
P.O. Box Central 25

Made in Europe

P.O.B. 174027
D-600 Frankfurt
West Germany

Taiwan International Trade

3rd Floor, 84 An Ho Road.
Taipei
Taiwan R.O.C.

Trade Channel

Helmholtzstraat 61
H-1098 Amsterdam
Netherlands

Trade Contacts in West African Countries Kogan Page Ltd

120 Pentonville Road
London N1
United Kingdom

Trade Media Ltd

P.O.B. 1786
Kowloon Central
Hong Kong

Singapore Trade & Industry

Times Publishing Sdm. Bldg.
422 Thomson Road
Singapore 11
Republic of Singapore

Reference List B

The Direct Marketing Association
Haymarket House, 1 Oxenden Street
London SW1Y 4EE
Tel 0171 321 2525

The Advertising Association
Abford House, 15 Wilton Road
London SW1V 1NJ
Tel 0171 828 2771

The Marketing Society Ltd
Stanton House, 206 Worple Road
London SW20 8PN
Tel 0181 879 3464

Reference List C

Ashley Designs Ltd
2 Debdale Road
Wellingborough
Northants NN8 5AA

Direct Response Media
Westminster House
Kew Road
Richmond
Surrey TW9 2ND

Direct Marketing Services
Berkley Court, High Street
Cheltenham
Glos GL52 6DA

MCD ADVERTSING lTD
Finland House, 56 Haymarket
London SWIY 4RN

Reference List D
List Rental Companies

Chartsearch Direct Ltd
Columbus House
28 Charles Square
London N1 6HT
Tel: 0171 417 0700

Mardev
151-153 Wardour Street
London W1V 3TB

NDL International Ltd
Port House, Square Rigger Row
Plantation Wharf
London SW11 3TY

Cheryl Nathan
29 Freuton Gdns
Cockfosters
Herts EN4 9LX

SAMPLES OF SOME DIRECT MARKETING ADS

NOW AVAILABLE...
WITHOUT A PRESCRIPTION!!!

SECOND CHANCE HAIR REVITALIZER

SECOND CHANCE STOPS HAIR LOSS

Our laboratory has developed a hair and scalp preparation that promotes hair growth. The ingredients contained in this product are all FDA approved and the non-prescription strength ensures safe topical application daily. This product revitalizes dormant and latent hair through the introduction of nutrient stimulants and nitrogen laden amino acids.

MILLIONS OF ANXIOUS PROSPECTS

Six out of every ten men have some hair loss. This is your market, not to mention the millions of women who hide their hair loss with wigs. Once you introduce SECOND CHANCE to your customer, they keep buying from you every 60 days, year after year as this product is not available in stores. You can set up your own wholesale distributorship or MLM company and buy at large-quantity big-discount prices.

MAKE BIG PROFITS ON EVERY SALE

Order a sample of SECOND CHANCE now at the wholesale price of $20.00; or start making big money and try our *INTRODUCTORY OFFER* of 10 bottles at $15.00 each. At the retail price of $39.95 you make 125% profit. ACT NOW!!

COPYRIGHT © 1986 LEE LABORATORIES

SUGGESTED
RETAIL PRICE
$39.95

...*Generous*
2 Month Supply!

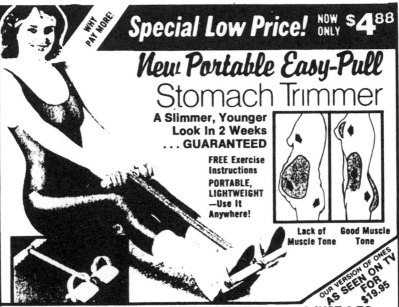

KEEPS YOUR HAIRDO IN PERFECT SHAPE WHILE YOU SLEEP!

Whatever your hair style . . . even elaborate bouffants . . . "Sleeping Beauty" Bonnet holds every hair in place! Special Velcro closure adjusts instantly.

ONLY $2⁸⁸

- At bedtime, gently slip "Sleeping Beauty" Bonnet over your hairdo; press ends firmly together in front.
- Sleep carefree all night long. Bonnet molds itself to your hairdo; cradles every hair in place.
- Take off bonnet in morning; and your hair looks like you've just walked out of the beauty parlor.

"Sleeping Beauty" Bonnet

Now, you need never again worry about messing up your hairdo while you sleep. Because now you can crush-proof your coiffure for the night — no matter how bouffant or elaborate the style . . . no matter how you may shift or squirm in your sleep!

Our ingenious "Sleeping Beauty" bonnet instantly molds itself to your hairdo; protects it all night long! Holds every hair in place — exactly the way you've combed or set it. Yet it's so lightweight and cool, it doesn't interfere with your sleep! And, any time you switch your hair style, "Sleeping Beauty" instantly reshapes itself to fit with the same firm, gentle protection!

Slip on in seconds; just press ends to lock in place for the night — with no slipping, sliding, or hair-mussing! Lightweight net is washable, folds to take up practically no room in purse or luggage when you travel! Order today.

SATISFACTION GUARANTEED
or your money happily refunded.

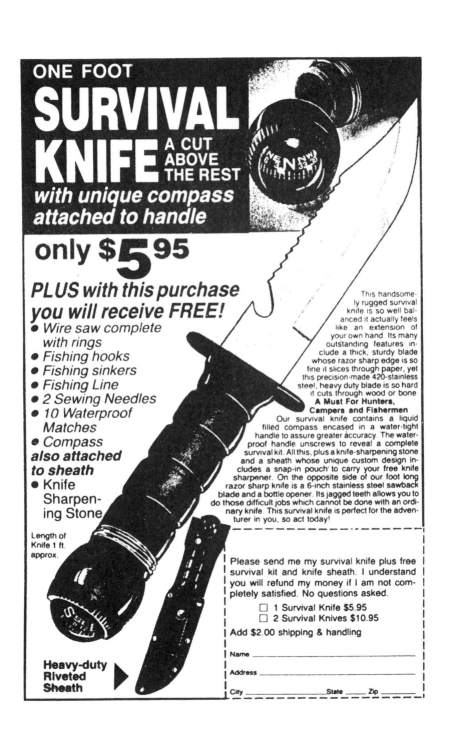

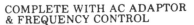

Coach's Jacket

RAINPROOF! WINDPROOF! The "weatherall" cover-up that's perfect anywhere - on the lake, at the ballgame, or for a quick dash to the market! Styled to fit both men and women! Outer shell is tightly woven nylon to **repel wind and rain!** Fleeced-flannel lining helps keep warmth in and cold out! Full-length snap front, elasticized cuffs, & drawstring bottom assure a snug, windproof fit. Two, side-cut pockets - great for packing tackle, pocketbook, snacks, and much more!

**Beat the Elements and Stay Warm!
Place Your Order Today!!**

NO HASSLE GUARANTEE

If you're not completely satisfied with your jacket(s), return them to us prepaid within 30 days for a FULL REFUND (less shipping & handling). Returned jacket(s) must be in original condition & container. If paying by check add 3-4 weeks for delivery.

*Checks can be processed in 48 hrs. if driver's license no., name, address, and phone no. appear on check.

**NOW
ONLY 11⁹⁵**

BUY MORE & SAVE MORE!!

1 Jacket - $11.95   2 Jackets - $23.00   3 Jackets - $34.00
Shipping & Handling: $3.00 Per Jacket

Name _____
Address _____
City/State _____ ZIP _____
Phone: Home ( ) _____
☐ My check or money order is enclosed.
☐ Charge to my: ☐ MasterCard   ☐ VISA   ☐ DISCOVER
Acct. No. _____
Expiration Date _____
Signature _____

Mail Check or Money Order Payable to

Q9

Total No. of Jackets _____
Total Jacket(s) Amount _____
Total Shipping & Handling _____
(WI residents add 5% state sales tax) _____
TOTAL AMOUNT _____

Mark your sizes and quantities!						
SIZES	S. 34-36	M. 38-40	L. 42-44	XL. 46-48	XXL. 50-52	XXXL. 54-56
Navy						

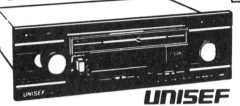